First
Facts

Insects

ELIZABETH COOPER

M
Macmillan

How to use this book

This book tells you lots of things about insects. There is a list of Contents on the next page. It shows you what each double page of the book is about. For example, pages 12 and 13 tell you about 'An insect's skin'.

On all of these pages there are some words which are printed in **bold** type. The bold type shows you that these words are in the glossary on pages 46 and 47. The glossary explains the meaning of some words which may be new to you.

At the very end of the book there is an index. The index tells you where to find certain words in the book. For example, you can use it to look up words like butterfly, pupa, caterpillar and many other words to do with insects.

Material used in this book first appeared in Macmillan World Library: *The Insect World*. Published by Macmillan Children's Books Houndmills, Basingstoke, Hampshire RG21 2XS and London Companies and representatives throughout the world

Designed by Julian Holland
Printed in Hong Kong

British Library Cataloguing in Publication Data
Cooper, Liz
Insects. — (First Facts). — (Macmillan world library).
1. Insects — Juvenile literature
I. Title II. Series
595.7   QL467.2
ISBN 0-333-46641-1

Contents

The busy world of insects 4

What is an insect? 6

Insect fossils 8

Different types of insect 10

An insect's skin 12

Wings, legs and feet 14

Eyes and feelers 16

How insects breathe and eat 18

The life cycle of an insect 20

Insects everywhere 22

Making a nest 24

Bees and wasps 26

Butterflies and moths 28

Jumping insects 30

Flies 32

Bugs and beetles 34

Pond insects 36

Shapes and colours 38

Insects in our homes 40

Insect pests 42

Our insect friends 44

Glossary 46

Index 48

The busy world of insects

Insects are everywhere on the Earth. Many are so small that we do not notice them. Some can live in places where other animals would not survive.

The hot springs in our picture are home for young **midges.** They are in Yellowstone Park in the United States of America.

bees storing food

busy leaf-cutter ants

Insects work hard. They use their feet and mouths for the special jobs they do. They build **nests.** They gather and store food. They feed their young. They must also keep safe from animals which like to eat them, especially the birds.

5

What is an insect?

Insects belong to a big group of animals called **arthropods.** Our picture shows how they fit into this group.

An arthropod is an animal with **joints** in its body and legs. The joints help it to move easily.

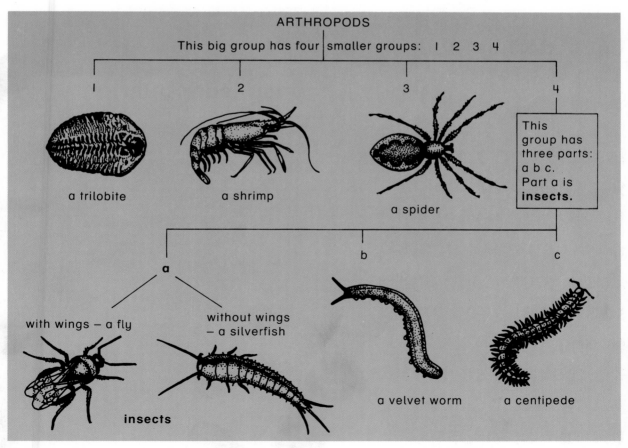

ARTHROPODS
This big group has four smaller groups: 1 2 3 4

1

2

3

4

a trilobite

a shrimp

a spider

This group has three parts: a b c. Part a is **insects.**

a

b

c

with wings – a fly

without wings – a silverfish

a velvet worm

a centipede

insects

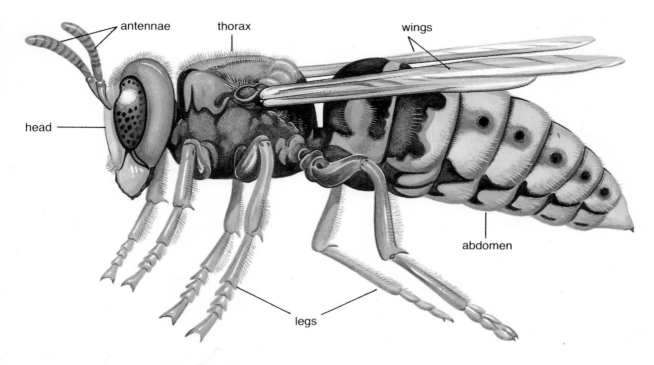

antennae

thorax

wings

head

abdomen

legs

the parts of an insect

Our picture shows the main parts of an insect – the head, the **thorax** and the **abdomen.**

Insects cannot keep warm in winter. They stay still like these ladybirds. In summer they warm up and move around.

ladybirds in winter

Insect fossils

Huge insects used to fly in **swamps** like this 300 million years ago. We know this because people have found remains of insects in rocks. These remains are called **fossils.**

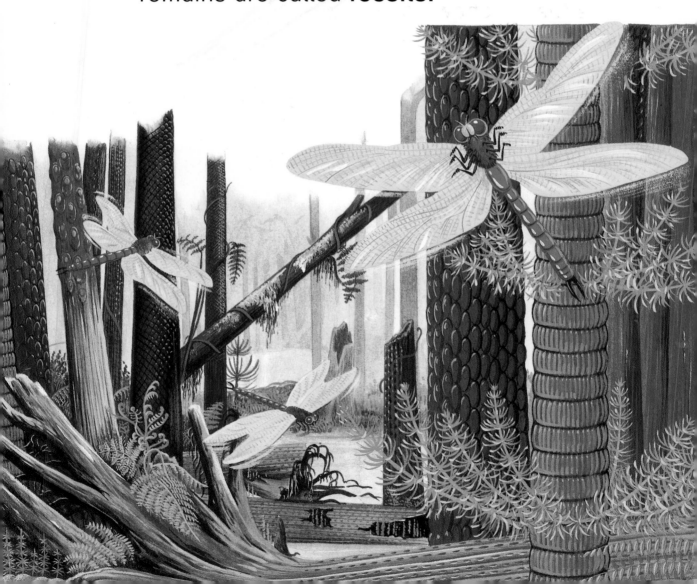

Some insect fossils have been found in a rock called **amber.**

Amber is the juice of pine trees which has gone very hard. Insects used to feed on the sticky juice and get caught in it.

These fossils show us that insects must have been living on Earth long before the dinosaurs and a very long time before humans.

an amber insect fossil

the insects' time on Earth

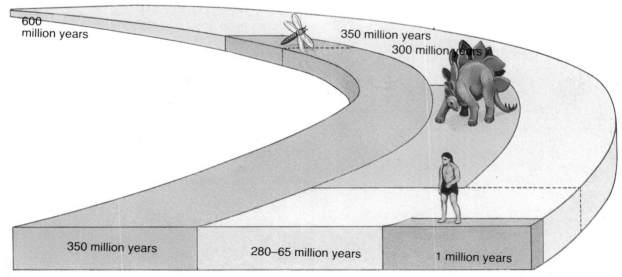

600 million years

350 million years
300 million years

350 million years

280–65 million years

1 million years

Different types of insect

Most insects live on or near plants. Plants give them their food and their shelter. Sometimes insects even look like parts of plants!

There are thousands of different types of plants and insects. The box below tells you where some different kinds of insect live.

Insects without wings	Where they live
Silverfish	in leaves and houses

Insects with wings (life cycle has three stages)	Where they live
Mayflies	larvae lie in water, adults fly free
Dragon flies and damselflies	larvae live in water adults fly free
Termites	in huge nests of soil
Grasshoppers and crickets	among plants
Leaf and stick insects	among plants

Insects with wings (life cycle has four stages)	Where they live
Lacewings and ant-lions	among plants and on the ground
Beetles	everywhere
Butterflies and moths	among plants
Bees, ants and wasps	among plants and on the ground

Sometimes insects need to change.

Some peppered moths changed their colour to black because their favourite trees had turned black from factory smoke.

Mosquitoes have become used to certain **poisons.** Now these poisons do not harm them.

two peppered moths – can you see the speckled one?

mosquitoes on a leaf

An insect's skin

a dragonfly with its new skin

An insect has a hard skin called an **exoskeleton.**

It comes off each time the insect grows. Underneath there is a nice new skin.

Can you see the dragonfly's old skin?

the middle part of an insect's body

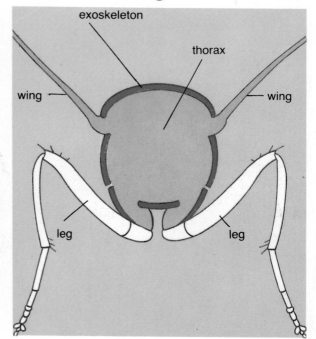

exoskeleton

thorax

wing

wing

leg

leg

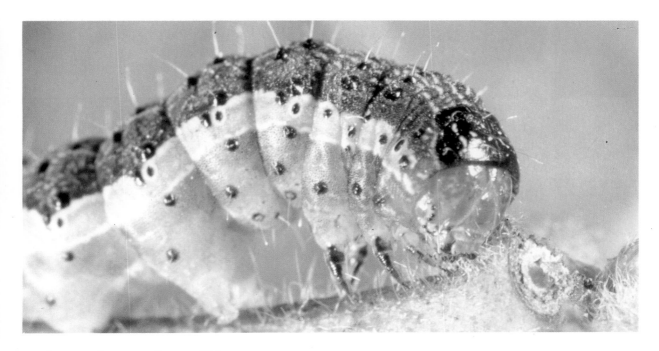

a bendy caterpillar

The body of an insect has many jobs to do.

The hard skin of an insect has hairs to help it feel, taste and smell things.

The hairs take messages to the insect's brain.

Its body is made of bits or segments joined together so it can bend in all directions.

hairs on a bee's leg

Wings, legs and feet

Wings help insects to fly away quickly from danger and to find their food. A wing is very strong because it is made of skin stretched over tubes called **veins.**

There are **muscles** in the insect's body which make the wing go up and down. When the wing goes up and down fast this makes the insect fly.

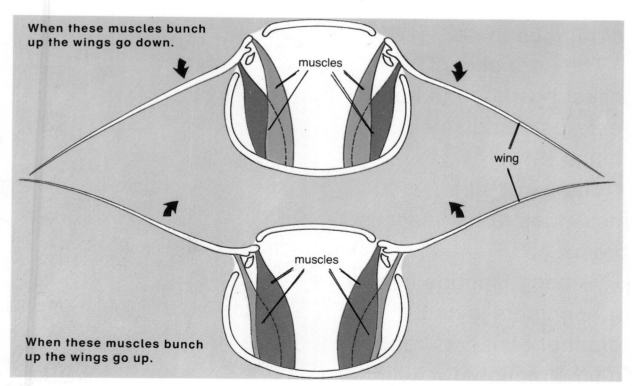

When these muscles bunch up the wings go down.

muscles

wing

muscles

When these muscles bunch up the wings go up.

a yellow underwing moth

An insect needs its legs and feet too.

It may use them for running or for swimming or for jumping.

A pond skater uses its long thin legs to walk on water.

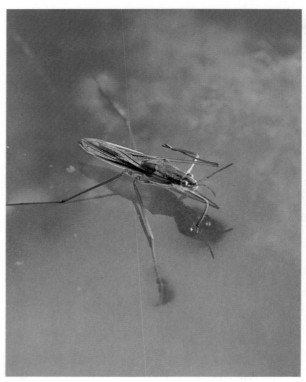

a pond skater on water

Eyes and feelers

Insects' eyes are different from ours.

Most young insects, called **larvae,** have several small eyes called simple eyes.

They cannot see shapes but they can tell night from day.

a compound eye

Most adult insects have two large eyes. These are called compound eyes.

They stick out from the insect's head so that it can see above, behind and below.

an insect can see all around

An insect feels, tastes and smells with the hairs on its body. Stiff hairs called bristles tell the insect where it is safe to go.

Instead of noses, insects have **antennae** with hairs for smelling. The antennae of this luna moth look rather like green feathers.

How insects breathe and eat

An insect does not have **lungs** like larger animals.

It has very small holes called spiracles on the sides of its body.

Air passes through the holes and along tubes inside the insect.

insects have holes for breathing

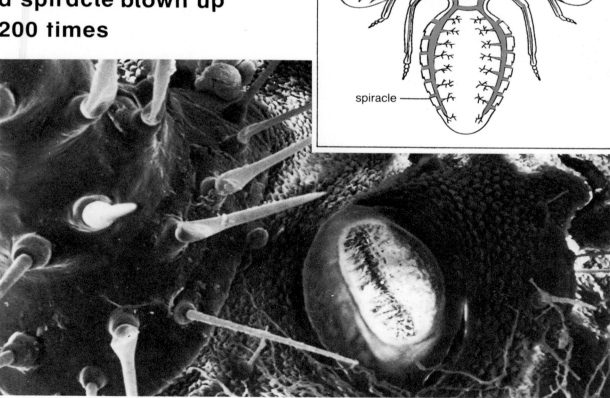

spiracle

a spiracle blown up 200 times

The insect uses **oxygen** from the air
to turn its food into energy.

It has a mouth to eat with. This
tiger beetle has very strong jaws
called mandibles. They have hard
pointed tips for cutting food. Most
insects eat plants or wood but some
eat **dung,** hair, skin or blood.

The life cycle of an insect

The way an insect changes and grows from an egg to an adult is called its life cycle. It can have three or four stages.

The young insect which comes out of the egg is called a **larva.** The grasshopper larva is called a nymph. It grows fast into an adult.

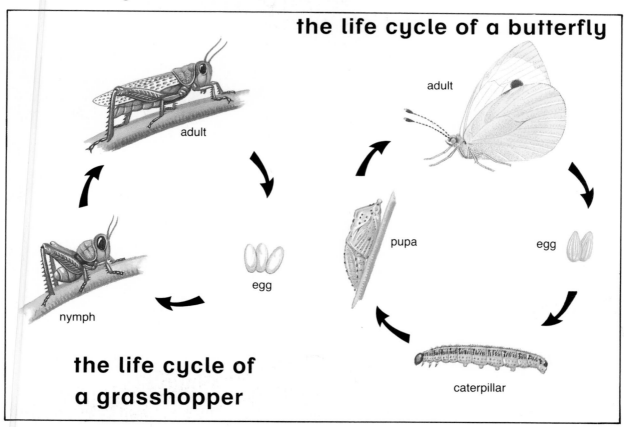

the life cycle of a butterfly

adult

egg

caterpillar

pupa

adult

nymph

egg

the life cycle of a grasshopper

A larva grows inside the insect egg. The butterfly larva is a caterpillar.

The caterpillar changes into a pupa. This is the resting stage for the insect to grow.

When the pupa opens, the adult insect, a butterfly, comes out.

butterfly eggs

honey-bee pupae

Insects everywhere

Insects live in some surprising places.

The ant-lion **larva** lives in sandy soil. It makes clever traps for ants.

The dune cricket lives in the desert. It has special feet to walk on the sand.

a dune cricket

ant-lion larva

Some insects can lay hundreds of
eggs at one time. If all of the eggs
grew into adults there would be too
many insects in the world.

Many insects are eaten by the
birds. If lots of them grow into adults
they may move in large groups and
eat a lot of food. This is called a
plague of insects.

Locusts eat all the leaves off the
farmers' crops.

Making a nest

Insects build their own **nests** or homes.
Many make their own building materials.

These weaver ants use the **larvae**
to make sticky silk thread for gluing
leaves together. You can see a
weaver ant holding a larva in the
middle of the picture.

**tunnels and
chambers inside an
ants' nest**

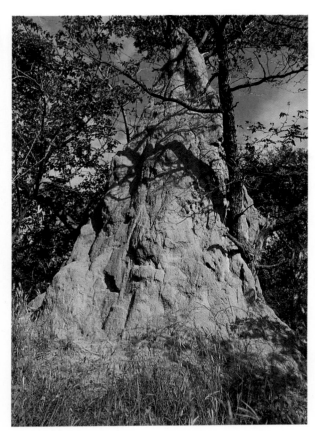

Many ants build a nest like a mound above ground.

Inside there are tunnels and spaces called chambers. In one chamber the **queen ant** lays eggs.

The **worker ants** take the eggs to other chambers where they hatch into larvae.

Bees and wasps

These honey-bees are inside a **hive.**
They are standing on nest **cells.** The
worker bees make the cells from **wax.**
   The **queen bee** has a red dot on
her. She is laying an egg in each nest
cell. The eggs will hatch into **larvae.**
The larvae are fed by the worker bees.

When the queen bee leaves the **nest** the workers go with her.

They go in a **swarm.** This swarm is resting on its way to a new nest.

Wasps build their nests from a kind of paper which they make by chewing wood into **pulp.**

a swarm of bees

a wasps' nest

Butterflies and moths

Look at the butterfly and the moth. Can you see how they are different?

a butterfly rests with wings closed

a moth rests with wings open

a butterfly wing

Butterflies fly during the day. Moths usually fly at night.

Their wings are covered in thousands of tiny **scales** which make up patterns.

The patterns help them to hide from their enemies.

Some butterflies are copy-cats and are called mimics.

They have the same patterns as poisonous butterflies, but they are not really poisonous at all.

a monarch butterfly caterpillar

Sometimes the patterns scare enemies away.

Some are like eyes which frighten the birds. Other patterns are a warning to birds.

The bright stripes of the caterpillar in the picture warn the birds that it is poisonous.

Jumping insects

Crickets, grasshoppers and locusts are all very good at jumping.

Grasshoppers make their sounds by rubbing their legs over a **vein** on the front wing.

Crickets rub the thick vein of one wing, called a file, over a bump on the other wing.

a grasshopper on a flower

insects making sounds

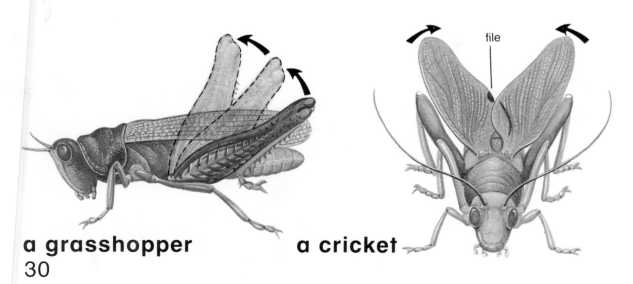

a grasshopper

a cricket

Locusts are big grasshoppers. They live in warm parts of the world. If there is plenty of food, very many locusts grow into adults. They eat every plant in their way.

The man in the picture is walking through a **swarm** of these noisy insects. There can be millions of them in one swarm.

Flies

There are many insects which we call flies, but a true fly only has one pair of wings.

All true flies have mouths which suck. Some have mouths like needles for feeding on blood. This is how the mosquito carries **disease.**

The fly here is a blowfly. Its eggs hatch into **larvae** called **maggots.**

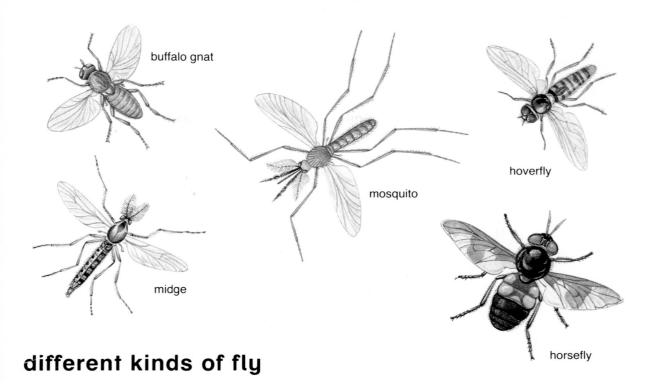

buffalo gnat

mosquito

hoverfly

midge

horsefly

different kinds of fly

Many flies bite. You can see some of them in the picture.

The names of flies can often tell you something about them. A hoverfly can hover and a horsefly bites horses.

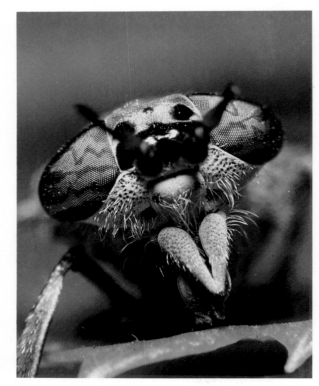

a horsefly's large eyes

33

Bugs and beetles

Bugs and beetles are not the same. Bugs have mouths like needles and beetles have biting mouths.

Many bugs such as greenfly feed on the juices of plants or trees. A few bugs feed on blood from animals and humans.

Some bugs feed on other insects. The assassin bug in the picture has caught a bee.

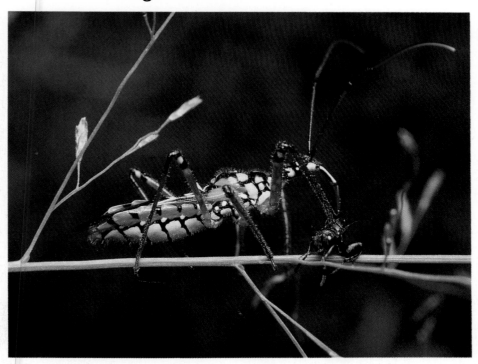

**two blister beetles on
a flower**

Most beetles eat plants
but the tiger beetle is
fierce and eats other
insects.
    Leave blister beetles
alone if you see any.
They can make your skin
come out in nasty blisters.

**a tiger beetle eating
a bug**

Pond insects

A pond is a home for many insects. The water contains small animals and plants which insects like to eat. Most of the insects in the water are **larvae.** The adults fly above the surface.

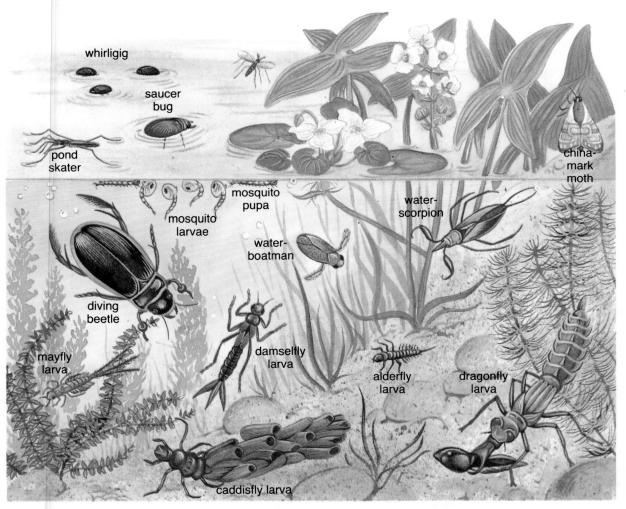

whirligig

saucer bug

pond skater

china-mark moth

mosquito pupa

mosquito larvae

water-scorpion

water-boatman

diving beetle

mayfly larva

damselfly larva

alderfly larva

dragonfly larva

caddisfly larva

36

an adult dragonfly

Can you see the dragonfly larva in
the pond picture? It is catching a
tadpole to eat.

When the larva is fully grown it will
leave the water and turn into a
beautiful dragonfly.

Some water insects dive and swim
very fast to catch other small
animals.

Shapes and colours

Insects try hard not to be eaten. Many have special shapes, colours or patterns. They match the plants or ground around them so they cannot be seen easily. This is called **camouflage.**

Stick and leaf insects are camouflaged to look just like sticks and leaves.

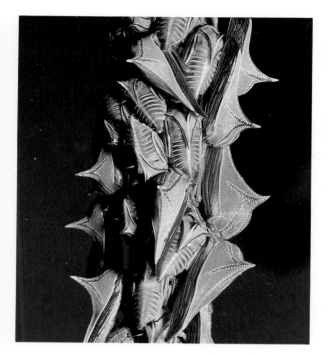

treehoppers or thornbugs

Other insects with a clever disguise are the treehoppers. They look just like sharp thorns, to trick the birds.

Sometimes male and female insects look very different. The male vaporer moth has big attractive wings.

The female has no wings at all. She spends her life laying eggs.

vaporer moths

female   male

Insects in our homes

Our houses make nice safe homes for many insects.

Insect **pests** like the silverfish have places to hide and plenty of food to eat.

a silverfish eating breadcrumbs

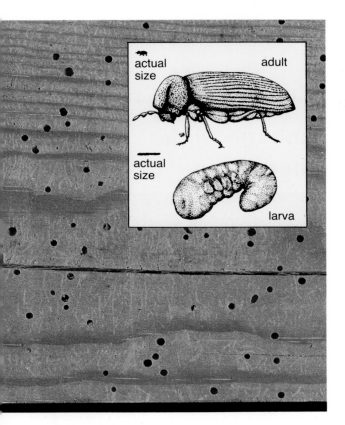

At night some insects come out of hiding.

The cockroach comes out to feed on bad food. It can pass on **germs** to fresh food.

It likes the dark. It runs away if a light is put on.

a woodworm and the holes it makes

cockroaches feeding

Many insects that live in our homes came by ship from other places.

The woodworm or furniture beetle is an insect which once lived in dead trees. Now it eats holes in our furniture.

41

Insect pests

Some insects like to eat our crops.

Cabbage white caterpillars eat our cabbages.

The Colorado beetle eats potatoes.

cabbage white caterpillars

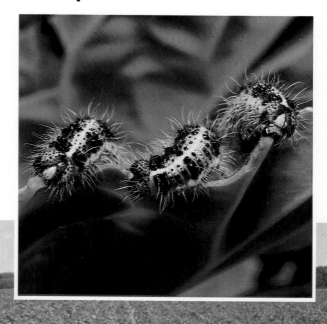

Colorado beetles have eaten these potatoes

The fly in our picture is called a
tsetse fly. It is feeding on human
blood. Tsetse flies in Africa carry a
disease called **sleeping sickness.**

Insect **pests** are a problem for us.
People have made some special
poisons which can kill the insects.

They are not very safe to use and
they do not always work.

A safer way of getting rid of them is
to get other insects to eat them.

Our insect friends

Some insects are our friends. This
hive of honey-bees is in an orchard.
The bees help the trees to make fruit.

44

Bees and other insects go to flowers to drink their **nectar.**

They pick up **pollen** on their feet and carry it to other flowers.

The pollen makes the flowers grow fruit or seeds.

Bees make **honey** and **wax** which we can use.

a silkworm's cocoon

Silkworms give us beautiful silk from their **cocoons.**

Some caterpillars in Australia helped people by eating a weed called the prickly pear cactus.

caterpillars on a prickly pear cactus

45

Glossary

abdomen the back part or tail of an insect.

amber the juice which came from pine trees millions of years ago and went very hard.

antenna a feeler on an insect's head. Each insect has two antennae which help it to smell.

arthropod an animal which has joints in its body and legs. It also has a hard outside skin. All insects are arthropods.

camouflage a special shape, colour or pattern which an insect has to match its surroundings. An insect with camouflage can hide from its enemies.

cell one small part of a bees' nest. There are hundreds of cells in a bees' nest. The bees make them from wax.

cocoon the case in which an insect grows.

disease an illness of a living animal or plant. Some insects can pass disease from one animal or human to another.

dung droppings from animals.

exoskeleton the hard skin of an insect.

fossil the remains of an animal or a plant, usually found in rock.

germ a tiny animal that causes disease.

hive a house for bees to live in. They make honey in the hive.

honey a sweet sticky liquid which bees make from the nectar of flowers. The bees store it in their nest.

joint the place where two parts of a body are joined. An insect has joints between the parts of its body and legs.

larva the second stage of an insect. The larva hatches out of an egg.

lung one of two parts of the body which an animal or human uses to breathe.

maggot the larva of a fly. It has no legs and moves by wriggling.

midge a tiny fly with two wings.

muscle a part of the body of an animal or human which makes another part to move.

nectar the sweet liquid in flowers. Bees and other insects feed on nectar.

nest a home which some insects make for themselves.

oxygen a part of the air which animals need in order to breathe.

pest an animal which is a nuisance to humans. Some pests eat the food we grow or the things in our homes.

poison a harmful liquid or powder which can kill plants or animals.

pollen a kind of powder in the centre of flowers.

pulp a soft mixture of chewed wood or plants and water.

queen ant a large female ant which lays eggs.

queen bee a large female bee which lays eggs.

scale one of the many tiny parts which cover the wing of a butterfly or moth.

sleeping sickness a serious disease which is passed on from cattle to humans by the tsetse fly in Africa.

swamp an area of wet muddy land sometimes covered in shallow water.

swarm a large number of insects all moving together on their way to find a new nest.

thorax the middle part of an insect. The legs and the wings are joined to the thorax so the thorax is important for movement.

vein one of the many tubes in an insect's wing. The veins make the wing strong.

wax a substance made by bees and used by them to make the walls of their nest cells.

worker ant a female ant which does many jobs. It looks after the eggs and the larvae.

worker bee one of the many female bees which do all the work inside and outside the hive.

Index

abdomen 7
alderfly larva 36
ant 5, 24, 25
antenna 17
ant-lion 22
arthropod 6

bee 5, 26, 27, 44, 45
beetle 19, 34, 35, 41, 42
bug 34, 36
butterfly 20, 21, 28, 29

caddisfly larva 36
camouflage 38
caterpillar 29, 42, 45
cockroach 41
cocoon 45
cricket 22, 30

dragonfly 12, 36, 37

egg 20, 21, 23, 26, 32

exoskeleton 12
eye 16

file 30
fly 32, 33, 43
fossil 8, 9

grasshopper 20, 30
greenfly 34

hive 26, 44
honey 45
hoverfly 33

ladybird 7
larva 21, 24, 25, 26, 32, 36, 37
leaf insect 38
life cycle 20
locust 23, 30, 31

maggot 32
mayfly 36
midge 4, 33
mosquito 11, 32, 33, 36
moth 11, 14, 15, 17, 28, 36, 39

nest 24, 25, 26, 27
nymph 20, 21

pollen 45
pond 36, 37
pond skater 15, 36
pupa 20, 21

scale 28
segment 13
silkworm 45
silverfish 40
spiracle 18
stick insect 38
swarm 27, 31

termite 25
thorax 7
treehopper 39
tsetse fly 43

wasp 27
water boatman 36
water scorpion 36
wax 45
whirligig 36
wing 14
woodworm 41

Acknowledgements
The Publishers wish to thank Rentokil and Shell for their invaluable assistance in the preparation of this book.
Photographic credits *(t=top b=bottom l=left r=right)*
4 ZEFA; 5*t* Stephen Dalton/NHPA; 5*b*, 7 Aquila; 9 Reproduced by permission of the Director, British Geological Survey (NERC); 11*t* Stephen Dalton/NHPA; 11*b*, 12 Aquila; 13*t* A Shell photograph; 13*b* Biophoto Associates/NHPA; 15*t*, 15*b* Stephen Dalton/NHPA; 16 Biophoto Associates/NHPA; 17 Anthony Bannister/NHPA; 18 Biophoto Associates/NHPA; 19 Keith Porter; 21*t* A Shell photograph; 21*b* Stephen Dalton/NHPA; 22 Anthony Bannister/NHPA; 23 A Shell photograph; 24 Ivan Polunin/NHPA; 25 Anthony Bannister/NHPA; 26, 27*t* Stephen Dalton/NHPA; 27*b*, 28/29 Aquila; 29*b* James Carmichael/NHPA; 30 Anthony Bannister/NHPA; 31 ZEFA; 32 Keith Porter; 33 G.J. Cambridge/NHPA; 34, 35*t* Anthony Bannister/NHPA; 35*b* Stephen Dalton/NHPA; 37 Anthony Bannister/NHPA; 38 Ivan Polunin/NHPA; 39 Aquila; 40*t* Stephen Dalton/NHPA; 40/41, 41*b* Rentokil; 42*t* Aquila; 42*b* A Shell photograph; 43 Anthony Bannister/NHPA; 44 Aquila; 45*t* Stephen Dalton/NHPA; 45*b* NHPA; cover and title page Stephen Dalton/NHPA